THE APPROACHING COAST

Marlatt

Bb Trumpet 1

THE APPROACHING COAST

David Marlatt

Bb Trumpet 2

THE APPROACHING COAST

David Marlatt

F Horn

THE APPROACHING COAST

David Marlatt

Trombone

THE APPROACHING COAST

David Marlatt

Tuba

THE APPROACHING COAST

David Marlatt